LETTERS MADE WITH LEAVES

Mariana Tchen

Dedication:

To all children who wonder
about nature

Aa
A
is for
apple

Bb

B is for
bird

C c

is for
cat

Dd

D is for

dinosaur

E e

E is for eye

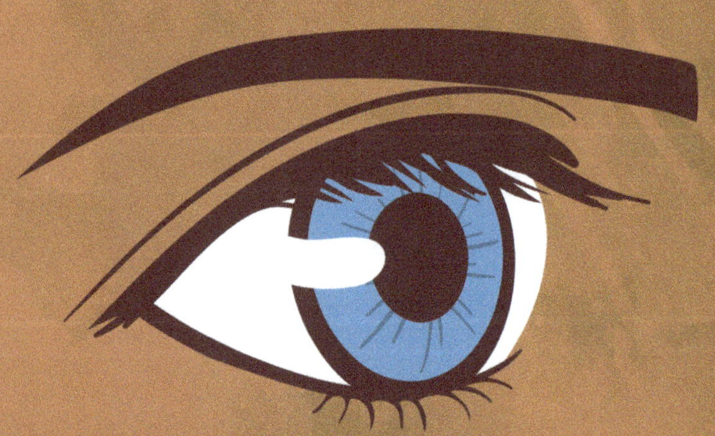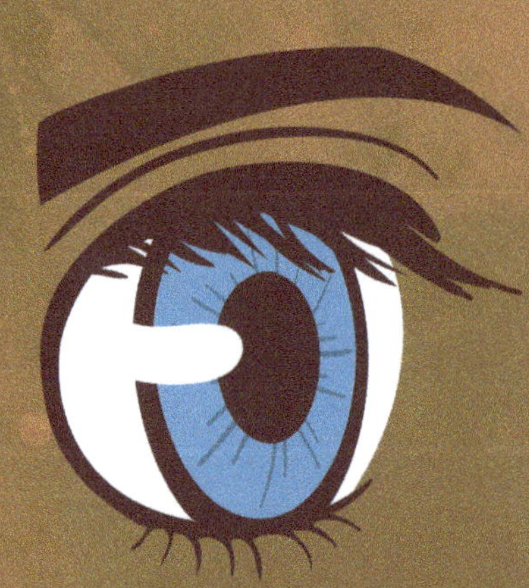

F f

F is for
fish

G g
G is for
guitar

H h

Ii

is for

icecream

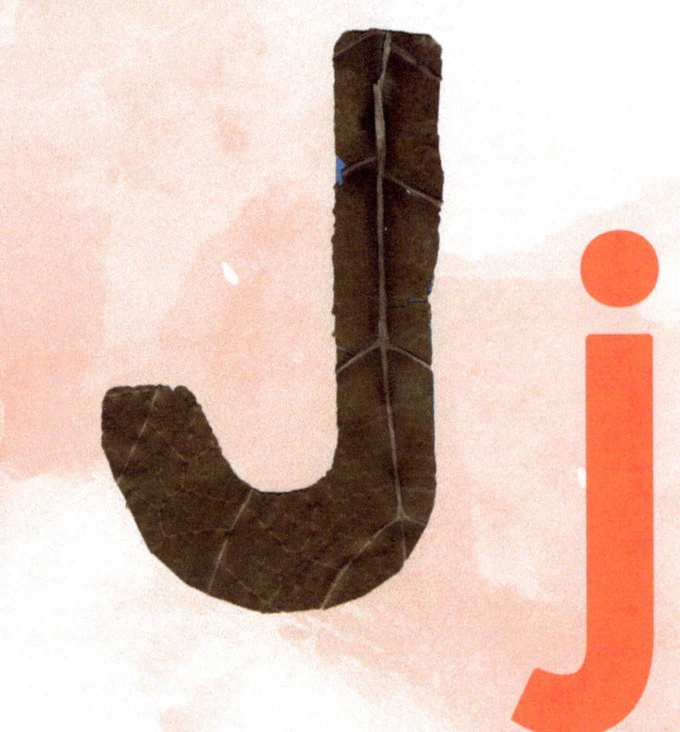

Jj

is for
juice

K k

k is for key

L l

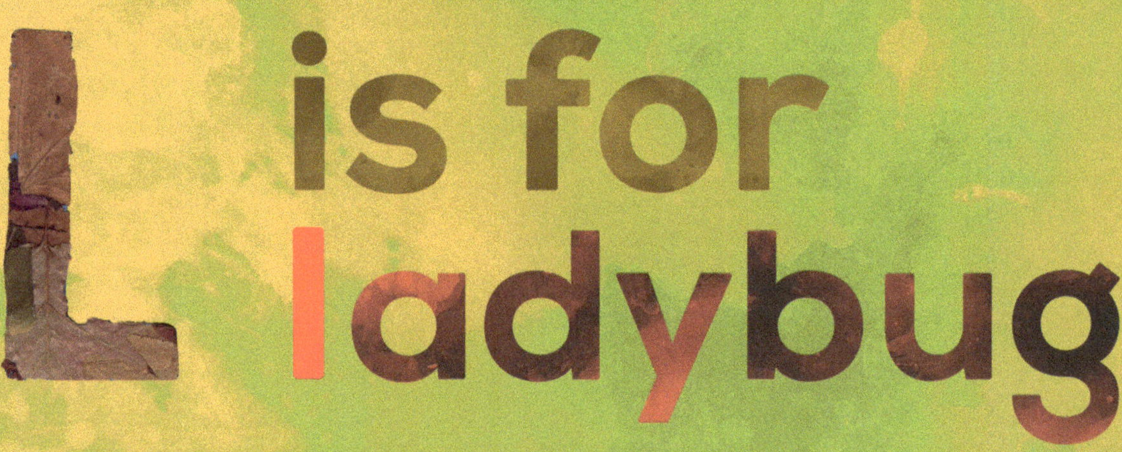

BE
HAPPY

M m

M is for maracas

N n
N is for
nose

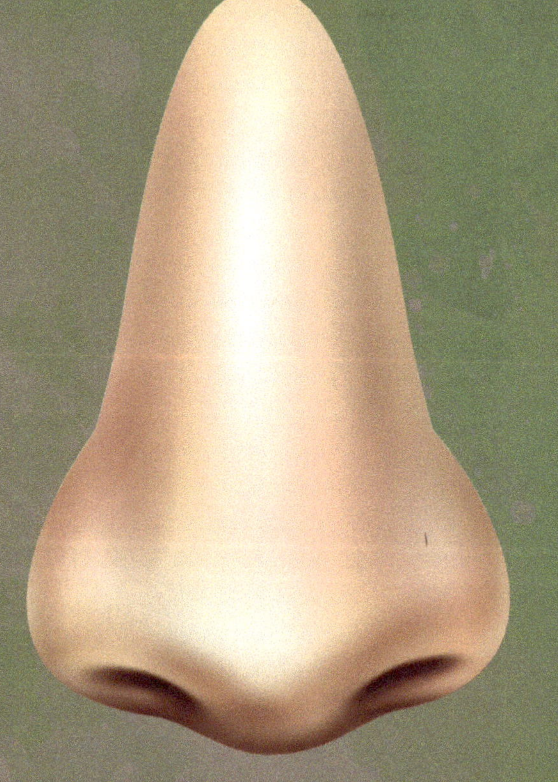

O o
is for
orange

P
P
p
is for
pen

Qq

q is for quilt

Rr

R is for rainbow

S s
S is for snake

T t

T is for
turtle

Uu
is for
up

V V
V is for
vase

W
W
W is for
wind

X x
is for
xylophone

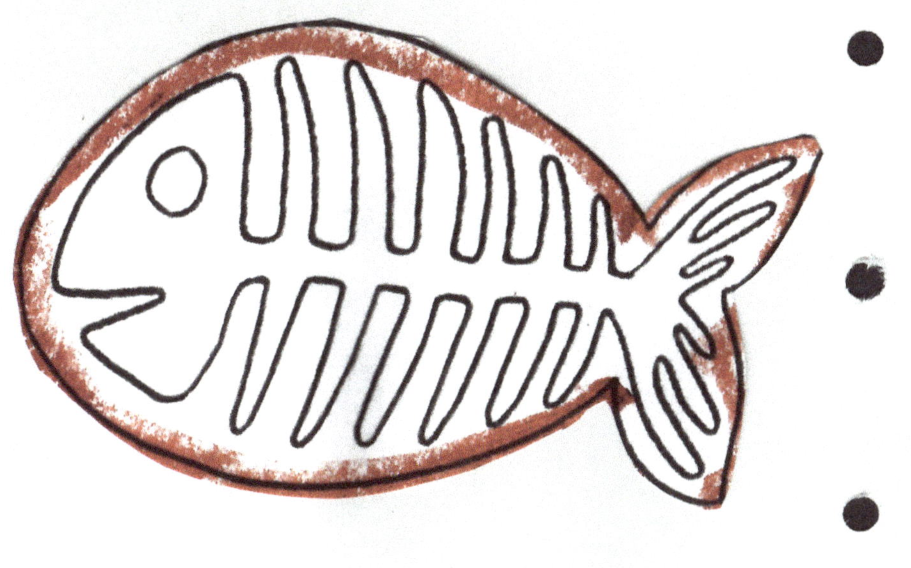

Y
Y
y
is for
yolk

Zz
z is for
zebra